LIFE DURING THE
CALIFORNIA
GOLD RUSH

by Bethany Onsgard

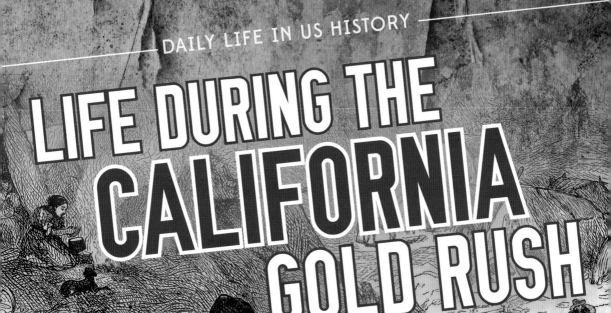

Content Consultant
John Putman
Associate Professor of History
San Diego State University

Core Library

An Imprint of Abdo Publishing
www.abdopublishing.com

www.abdopublishing.com

Published by Abdo Publishing, a division of ABDO, PO Box 398166,
Minneapolis, Minnesota 55439. Copyright © 2015 by Abdo Consulting
Group, Inc. International copyrights reserved in all countries. No part of
this book may be reproduced in any form without written permission from
the publisher. Core Library™ is a trademark and logo of Abdo Publishing.

Printed in the United States of America, North Mankato, Minnesota
092014
012015

Cover Photo: North Wind Picture Archives/AP Images
Interior Photos: North Wind Picture Archives/AP Images, 1; Jay Boivin/
Thinkstock, 4; Library of Congress, 7; Red Line Editorial, 9, 37; North Wind
Picture Archives, 12, 20, 26, 28, 30, 42; Photos.com/Thinkstock, 15, 23,
45; Bettmann/Corbis, 17, 25; J. Gurney & Son/Library of Congress, 33; AP
Images, 34; Ricky Barnard/Thinkstock, 39; iStock Editorial/Thinkstock, 40

Editor: Lauren Coss
Series Designer: Becky Daum

Library of Congress Control Number: 2014944227

Cataloging-in-Publication Data
Onsgard, Bethany.
 Life during the California Gold Rush / Bethany Onsgard.
   p. cm. -- (Daily life in US history)
 ISBN 978-1-62403-624-8 (lib. bdg.)
 Includes bibliographical references and index.
 1. California--Gold discoveries--Juvenile literature.   2. California--Gold
discoveries--Social aspects--Juvenile literature.   3. Gold mines and mining--
California--1846-1850--Social aspects--Juvenile literature.   I. Title.
 979.4--dc23
                                                    2014944227

CONTENTS

CHAPTER ONE

GOLD!

What do you picture when you think of California? Today, the state is known for sunny beaches, movie stars, and rows of palm trees. But in the early 1800s, California was a very different place. It was home to more than 100,000 Native Americans. Many Spanish settlers also lived in the area. They had been building missions in California since the 1700s. But most of the land was

Spanish settlers built many missions in California in the 1700s. There they attempted to convert Native Americans to Christianity.

49ers

San Francisco's football team is named after the many men and women who made the long journey to California in 1849. So many people rushed to the West Coast during this year, the first year after gold was found, that the world created a nickname for them—the 49ers. When the team was formed in 1946, its founder wanted a name that honored California's wild beginnings. The 49ers' original logo was a gold miner in boots jumping and shooting a gun.

wilderness. California was not yet a state. It had no big cities, only small settlements. Even San Francisco, now one of the biggest cities in California, was a small fishing and shipping town. But all of that began to change in 1848.

Marshall's Big Find

Before California was known for gold, it was famous for another natural resource—trees. Many settlers worked at sawmills. They cut and shipped lumber to use for construction and firewood. One of these workers was James W. Marshall. He worked at Sutter's Mill, a sawmill near what is now Sacramento, California.

Marshall stands in front of Sutter's Mill, where he found gold in 1848.

On January 24, 1848, Marshall was walking near the American River when he spotted something shiny in the water. It was gold. At first, many people doubted Marshall. They thought the gold claims were just rumors. But soon newspapers began to confirm that California was gold country.

Gold was a valuable resource. Many goods were made from it. It could also be used to purchase goods and services. Gold was an accepted form of currency around the world. In December 1848, President James Polk announced the discovery of gold in his State of the Union speech. Sutter's Mill became known as the birthplace of the California Gold Rush.

A Long Journey

News of the gold in California spread. Soon prospectors from across the United States began making their way west to hunt for gold. There were two main ways people traveled to California from the eastern United States. Many traveled over the land. Others traveled by sea, usually sailing around the tip of South America. It was not an easy or quick trip. Both routes took nearly six months.

To get west by land, many miners and their families traveled on the California Trail. The trail ran from Missouri to California. Miners traveled on foot or by wagon. Anything they couldn't carry was left behind. They rode over rugged land, and they faced starvation and thirst.

The Long Journey to California

This map shows the most popular routes that Americans living in the East took to reach California. Some settlers opted for the more expensive but quicker Panama shortcut. Prospectors sailed down to Panama, which they crossed on land. Then they sailed up to California. If you were traveling from where you live, what route would you take? What are the pros and cons of each route?

Traveling to California by sea was equally difficult. Travelers faced months of rough water, with few activities to do. Many people became seasick or ill from the diseases that spread quickly in the ships' close quarters. Travelers couldn't pack fruits and vegetables because they would get rotten on such a long journey. However, travelers were exposed to new cultures when ships made stops in Central and South America to restock supplies.

No matter which route miners chose, they risked a lot to get to California. For some prospectors, the risk paid off. Tales of the huge quantities of gold spread across the globe. Before long, fortune seekers were traveling from around the world. People were arriving in California by the thousands only a few months after the discovery at Sutter's Mill. By 1849, the great California Gold Rush had begun.

President Polk's 1848 State of the Union Address helped convince many Americans that there was actually gold in California. In the speech, Polk talks about how valuable the territory of California is:

> It was known that mines of the precious metals existed to a considerable extent in California at the time of its acquisition. Recent discoveries render it probable that these mines are more extensive and valuable than was anticipated. The accounts of the abundance of gold in that territory are of such an extraordinary character as would scarcely command belief were they not corroborated by the authentic reports of officers in the public service who have visited the mineral district and derived the facts which they detail from personal observation. . . . The explorations already made warrant the belief that the supply is very large and that gold is found at various places in an extensive district of country.
>
> Source: "1848 State of the Union Address." Historic Speeches. Presidential Rhetoric, n.d. Web. Accessed May 22, 2014.

What's the Big Idea?

Take a close look at this speech. What is Polk's main point about the value of the West? Pick out two details he uses to make this point. What can you tell about the importance of the gold rush based on this speech?

CHAPTER TWO

A MINER'S LIFE

After trudging across the wilderness or braving dangerous seas, the hard work wasn't over. Mining was a physically demanding job. Prospectors worked 12- to 16-hour days, six days a week. They spent most of the day shoveling heavy dirt and rock.

Once they arrived in California, miners faced backbreaking work. Many went home empty-handed.

Female Gold Miners

Prospectors are almost always depicted as bearded, dust-covered men. But some pioneering women also tried their hand at looking for gold. One of the most famous female miners was Elsa Jane Guerin. She left her husband and children behind in Saint Louis, Missouri, to enter the goldfields. After a few months in gold country, she returned home to her family a very rich woman. Charlotte "Charley" Parkhurst also found success during the gold rush years. Although she tried her hand in the goldfields, Parkhurst found a more stable career as a stagecoach driver. She spent most of her life disguised as a man.

Panning for Gold

When gold was first discovered in 1848, it could often be seen glimmering at the bottom of rivers. To access the gold, miners used a technique called panning. Miners swirled mud from a river in a pan. If the miners were lucky, gold would appear. Gold is heavier than mud. This meant any bits of gold would separate from the dirt and fall to the bottom of the pan.

All the easy-to-find gold was soon mined. Then miners needed

Prospectors shovel dirt into a Long Tom, hoping to spot flecks of gold.

to access the gold hidden deeper in the rivers. To do this, they used a tool called a Long Tom. The Long Tom was shaped like a seesaw. It had a slotted bottom, just like a gold pan. But it took many miners to operate it. Men would shovel dirt and gravel into the machine. Then the miners rocked it back and forth until all of the debris fell away. With luck, only gold would remain.

Eventually, even the Long Tom wasn't enough to find the gold hidden in the earth. By 1850 much of the surface gold was gone. As the surface gold disappeared, prospectors had to work harder to continue bringing in money.

The miners began digging even deeper. They sometimes diverted entire rivers to mine the riverbeds. They took pickaxes to the hillsides. Larger mining operations used a process called hydraulic mining. They sprayed thousands of gallons of water down hillsides. The water washed away trees and sediment. Miners hoped to find gold under the surface.

Gold Mining and Nature

New inventions in mining technology were good news for the men and women who went west. However, the new techniques devastated California's natural landscape. Hydraulic mining cleared massive forests of oak and pine. The hillsides were left bare. When it rained, these hillsides were washed away by water. Towns downstream were hit by enormous floods of mud. The water was also contaminated. Water supplies were poisoned with mercury, arsenic, cyanide, and other toxic substances from mining tools.

Although few women came west during the California Gold Rush, many who did found work washing clothes and cooking for the miners.

Women in the Gold Rush

While some families made the journey out west together, most of the people who rushed to California were men. Women made up less than 10 percent of California's population in 1850. Most married prospectors planned to return home once they had made their fortunes. Others hoped to send for their wives and children once they were settled. In the meantime, the miners' wives would run the miners' farms and businesses back home.

However, many of these miners weren't used to housekeeping work. They often didn't know how to do their own laundry. Some couldn't even cook for themselves.

When the women who lived in California saw this, they found their own gold mine. California needed journalists, hatmakers, saloon entertainers, and shopkeepers. Women rose to the call. Women began charging high prices for the work they had been doing for their families and in their homes. One woman made $18,000 just by baking pies. Most men lived in mining camps. But many missed the comforts of home. Women opened and ran boardinghouses near the mining camps where the miners could stay. They provided the miners with meals, housekeeping, and a place to sleep.

The excerpt below from a diary entry shows what Indiana woman Margaret Frink heard about California:

> Mrs. McKinney had a nephew who went to California in 1849, and she told me of the wonderful tales of the abundance of gold that she had heard: "that they kept flour-scoops to scoop the gold out of the barrels that they kept it in, and that you could soon get all you needed for the rest of your life. And as for a woman, if she could cook at all, she could get $16.00 per week for each man that she cooked for, and the only cooking required to be done was just to boil meat and potatoes and serve them on a big chip of wood, instead of a plate, and the boarder furnished the provisions." I began at once to figure up in my mind how many men I could cook for, for there should be no better way of making money.

> Source: Joann Levy. They Saw the Elephant: Women in the California Gold Rush.
> Hamden, CT: Archon Books, 1990. Print. 92.

Point of View

This passage talks about one woman's view of the gold rush. How did the roles of women and men compare in California during the gold rush decade? Were there as many opportunities for women as there were for men? How might life have been different for women and men in California at the time?

CHAPTER THREE

FACES OF THE GOLD RUSH

The gold rush drew people not only from across the United States but also from around the world. Most of the first miners came from California. The area had previously been controlled by Mexico, which had been controlled by Spain until 1821. As a result, many Spanish-Mexican settlers, known as Californios, were already living in California. Many made their way to the goldfields. Mexicans, Chileans, and Peruvians

The California Gold Rush drew prospectors from all over the globe.

Slavery in the West

The majority of the African Americans who came to California were free citizens seeking wealth for themselves. However, some white slave owners from Southern states brought slaves with them on their journey to the West. Slaves had no hope of the golden payoffs the free miners could earn. However, many miners opposed slavery. Miners with slaves had free labor. The other miners believed slaves gave miners an unfair advantage. Soon gold rush territory became an area where slavery was unpopular. When California became a state in 1850, it entered the Union as a free state. That meant slavery was illegal.

arrived by the end of fall 1848. As word continued to spread, prospectors came from even farther distances. Eventually they came from across the country and around the world.

African-American Miners

In 1848 slavery was legal in many Southern US states. However, some African Americans lived freely in Northern states where slavery was outlawed. Free or slave, African Americans faced challenges. Many African Americans headed west in

Some African Americans were brought as slaves to California, where they worked in the goldfields for their owners.

search of fortune in California. They hoped to escape the legacy of slavery. These prospectors found some new opportunities. But they experienced much of the same racism and discrimination that they had back east.

Immigrants from China

By the 1850s, miners were flooding in from across the globe. They came from Australia, Great Britain, and France, as well as from other European countries.

Chinese miners made up the largest group of foreign immigrants to come to California.

Chinese merchants loaned many Chinese immigrants money for their travel expenses. Once they arrived in California, money was taken from the immigrants' wages until their debt was paid off. However, because of interest rates, most immigrants had to pay off much more than the original loan. The Chinese population had exploded by the time the rush ended in the late 1850s. By 1870 more than 63,000

Foreign Miners Tax

One of the most glaring examples of racism in California during the gold rush was the Foreign Miners Tax. This monthly tax, which started at $20, was imposed on any non-US miner. The tax was equal to more than $600 in today's currency. The tax affected Chinese immigrants the most. Many were still in debt from their journey to California and could not afford to pay the tax. The Chinese population was so large in California that between 1850 and 1870, Chinese contributions to the tax made up almost a quarter of the state's revenue.

Chinese immigrants work in the California goldfields.

Chinese immigrants lived in the United States. And 77 percent of those called California home.

Impact on Native Americans

Not everyone who lived in California during the gold rush hoped to seek riches. Many groups faced challenges and discrimination. But none fared worse than the Native Americans in the area.

Native Americans had been living in California for thousands of years before the first miner arrived. As more miners began arriving, they built mining camps on Native American land. The Native Americans

As settlers flooded into California hoping to strike it rich, they displaced thousands of Native Americans who lived there.

resisted losing their land. A violent cycle of conflicts began between the Native Americans and the miners. The miners usually won.

Skirmishes between the two groups continued throughout the 1850s. The Native American population declined quickly. Before the gold rush, the Native American population was more than 150,000. Within 20 years, it had been greatly reduced. By 1858, there were only approximately 30,000 Native Americans still left in California.

New Enterprises

With so many cultures in one place, the tension was high. But the newly arrived cultures and races forever changed the face of California. The prospectors brought with them new ideas, new customs, and new ways of life. As many as 50 different languages might be spoken in one mining camp. California continues to be a state shaped by its diversity, and much of that diversity originated during the gold rush years.

FURTHER EVIDENCE

There is a lot of information about Native Americans in Chapter Three. What is one of the main points of this chapter? What key evidence supports this point? Check out the article on Native Americans at the website below. Find a quote from the website that supports the chapter's main point. Does the quote support an existing piece of evidence in the chapter? Or does it add a new one?

Native Americans in the Gold Rush

www.mycorelibrary.com/gold-rush

CHAPTER FOUR

DAILY LIFE

During the California Gold Rush, hundreds of thousands of miners moved to California. They came as quickly as their horses or boats could carry them. In March 1848, there were approximately 157,000 people in the California territory. Fewer than 800 of these were US settlers. The rest were Native Americans and Californios. By the end of 1849, the number of US settlers had soared to more than

Although prospectors worked hard in the goldfields, they found time to relax and enjoy themselves.

Mining towns sprang up quickly in California during the gold rush years.

100,000. It was one of the biggest mass migrations in US history. In the mid-1850s, one in every 90 people in the United States was living in California.

Shopping

New mining towns, known as boomtowns, sprang up almost overnight. People arrived so quickly that towns weren't always ready for them. Everyday items, such as food and clothes, were hard to find. Small shops were built as fast as possible. But they weren't stocked with all of the goods people were used to. With so much demand for their goods, shopkeepers could charge outrageous prices. In today's money, a single egg could cost as much as $25. Coffee went for more than $100 per pound. In 1849 California, even a worn-out pair of boots could cost you more than $2,500 in today's prices.

Clothing

Although successful miners had money to spend, not many miners spent time or money on their appearance. If you walked into a gold rush mining town, you'd see most men dressed in baggy brown pants and shirts. Floppy hats

Gold Dust

The West was mostly uninhabited wilderness when miners rushed out to find gold. There were no banks like we're used to today. This meant that people couldn't always use coins or dollars for sales or transactions. Instead, people used gold dust as currency. In 1849, when gold dust was plentiful, a pinch was equal to $1. To pay someone, a miner could plunge his hand into a sack of gold and pull out a handful of gold dust worth $4 to $8. Eventually, as more banks were established, miners could turn in their gold to banks in exchange for banknotes. These were treated like coins.

Lotta Crabtree

Most gold rush saloons offered entertainment, usually dancing. Lotta Crabtree was one of the most famous dancers of the California Gold Rush. Lotta and her family arrived in California from New York in 1853, when she was only six years old. Her family ran a boardinghouse. The family met Lola Montez, a famous saloon performer. Montez began training Lotta to dance. In 1855 Lotta had her first performance at a mining camp. She was a hit. Soon Lotta was performing in saloons in different mining towns across California. Eventually she became so popular that she traveled east and became a famous stage performer.

protected them from the sun. Most men stopped shaving or cutting their hair. They had long, scraggly beards. Some prospectors claimed that with so few women around, they had no reason to look nice.

Entertainment

Miners worked hard. But when they weren't working, they looked for places to relax and have fun. Saloons were popular gathering places during the gold rush. At the saloons, miners would play cards or gamble.

Lotta Crabtree was a popular saloon performer during the California Gold Rush.

As mining towns grew bigger, they offered more options for entertainment. In October 1849, the Eagle Theater opened in Sacramento in a wood-and-canvas house. The first play it showed was called *The Bandit Chief*. Hundreds of miners came out to see the play. They paid more than $120 per ticket in today's money. Soon more theaters began cropping up across gold country, offering a wide range of entertainment.

CHAPTER FIVE

IMPACTS

By around 1858, the California Gold Rush was slowing down. The land had been stripped of valuable materials. Many miners packed up to head back home. Others found new careers and settled down. The miners who chose to stay began creating the state we know today.

The gold rush forever changed California and paved the way for its path to statehood.

The End of Mining

Historians estimate that around 12 million ounces (340 million g) of gold was mined during the gold rush. That would be worth around $20 billion using today's prices. When the amount of gold mined lessened in the late 1850s, miners had to find other ways to make a living. Many men saw another opportunity. California had warm weather, healthy soil, and a long growing season. Before long, miners were leaving goldfields for farm fields. These farmers provided fresh fruits and vegetables for the growing California

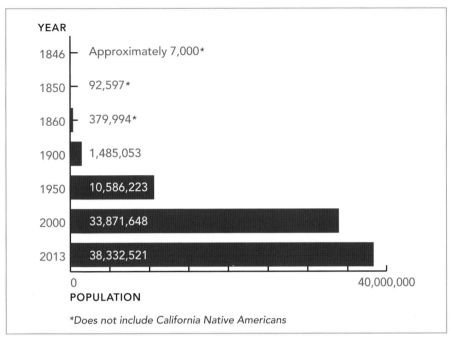

YEAR	POPULATION
1846	Approximately 7,000*
1850	92,597*
1860	379,994*
1900	1,485,053
1950	10,586,223
2000	33,871,648
2013	38,332,521

*Does not include California Native Americans

California's Population

The graph above shows how California's population changed. How does seeing this graph help you understand the information about California's population growth that you read in the book? Why might the population have continued growing even after the gold rush slowed?

population. They set the state's current economy in motion. Today, California produces almost half of US-grown fruits, nuts, and vegetables.

Population Boom and New Cities

Before the gold rush, California was mostly rural farmland and open wilderness. But when people began arriving by the thousands, they created new cities and towns. Some of these small towns became big cities, such as Sacramento and San Diego. San Francisco was one of the fastest-growing cities. As the closest port to the goldfields, it was the first California town many miners saw after their long sea journey. When gold was first discovered, San Francisco was a small town of roughly 1,000 people. It was little more than a settlement of canvas tents and wooden shacks. As the rush slowed, people moved out of the goldfields and back to the cities. By 1860 San Francisco's population was more than 56,000. As more people moved into the city, new buildings, roads, and businesses were built.

Ghost Towns

The gold rush helped create some of the biggest cities in California, but it also left some mining towns completely bare. When goldfields were emptied, prospectors left the mining towns in search of new work and more gold. The areas they left behind became known as ghost towns. Many of these towns are preserved and open to the public.

The ghost town of Bodie, California, was built in the 1850s, when gold was discovered in the area. By the 1920s, nearly all the town's residents had left.

California Becomes a State

The gold rush was also the key to California's statehood. With a huge population boom, along with the huge amounts of gold being unearthed, the US government was eager to make California a state. To be considered for statehood, an area needed to have a population of at least 60,000 US settlers. Before the gold rush, there were fewer than 1,000 US settlers in the state. California's population growth was so slow

Every year in late summer, Sacramento remembers the gold rush with its Gold Rush Days celebration.

that it could have taken decades to reach 60,000. But in 1850, only two years after gold was found at Sutter's Mill, California had 92,000 US settlers. It was admitted as the thirty-first US state. Neighboring West Coast states didn't have the same population push. It took them many more years to achieve statehood. Oregon became a state in 1859 and Washington in 1889.

The Golden State

The California Gold Rush drew people from across the country and around the world. People of all different backgrounds and cultures flocked to the region, helping make California the diverse state it is today. The miners' adventurous spirit is what many Californians are still known for. The California Gold Rush made a lasting impression on the West Coast's population and economy. It's no accident that California's nickname is still "The Golden State."

EXPLORE ONLINE

The focus of Chapter Five is the impact of the California Gold Rush. The website below also focuses on the gold rush's impacts. As you know, every source is different. How is the information given in the website different from the information in this chapter? What information is the same? How do the two sources present information differently? What can you learn from this website?

Effects of the Gold Rush
www.mycorelibrary.com/gold-rush

A DAY IN THE LIFE

James is a prospector who works in the goldfields of California. He traveled to the West alone, leaving his wife and children at home until he got settled.

5:00 a.m.
James wakes up and gets ready for work. Days start early for miners. He puts on his dusty brown work clothes, the same ones he's been wearing for months.

5:30 a.m.
Breakfast is served at the boardinghouse where James is staying. He eats a meal of bread and beans.

6:00 a.m.
The miners gather at the goldfields. They spend the morning shoveling mud and dirt from the river into a Long Tom.

12:00 p.m.
Lunchtime. Each day around noon, a woman comes by the goldfields. She brings homemade lunches for the miners to buy.

6:00 p.m.
After 12 hours of work, James and the other miners are finally done for the day. James packs up his shovel and heads back to the boardinghouse.

6:30 p.m.
James stops in at a small shop in the mining town. This is where mail for the miners is delivered. A letter is waiting for him from his wife, with updates about the family.

7:00 p.m.
Dinner is served at the boardinghouse.

8:00 p.m.
James heads to the saloon, a building with a few tables and a piano. Most of the miners gather here in the evenings. James and the other men spend the rest of the evening listening to music and playing cards.

STOP AND THINK

Tell the Tale

Chapter Two talks about women who chose to join men in the rivers, mining for gold. Write 200 words that tell the story of a woman working in the goldfield. Describe the sights and sounds of the river. What might she be thinking about while she works? Be sure to set the scene, develop a sequence of events, and offer a conclusion.

Dig Deeper

After reading this book, what questions do you still have about the many cultures that were represented during the California Gold Rush? Do you want to know about the customs or ideas they brought to the United States? Write down one or two questions that can guide you while doing research. Then write down a few sentences about your research and what you learned.

Say What?

Learning about life from a different era can mean learning words that are unfamiliar. Find five words in this book that you've never seen or heard before. Use a dictionary to find out what they mean, and write the meanings in your own words. Then use each new word in a sentence.

Surprise Me

Chapter Four discusses what daily life in California mining towns was like. What two facts about living on the West Coast during the gold rush did you find surprising? Why did you find them surprising? Write a few sentences about each fact.

GLOSSARY

banknote
a paper note a bank issues that can be used as regular money

Californio
a person living in California of Spanish-Mexican descent

currency
the money that a specific country uses

hydraulic
operated by pressure transmitted when a quantity of liquid is forced through a small hole or tube

interest
a fee for borrowing money

mission
a religious and military building built by Spanish settlers in California

prospector
a person who searches for mineral deposits, such as gold

revenue
income produced by a business or another moneymaking source

saloon
a place with beverages and often entertainment where people can socialize

sediment
material such as stones and sand deposited by water, wind, or glaciers

skirmish
a fight or a dispute

toxic
poisonous

LEARN MORE

Books

Dunn, Joe. *The California Gold Rush.* Edina, MN: Magic Wagon, 2008.

Fradin, Dennis B. *The California Gold Rush.* New York: Marshall Cavendish, 2009.

Holub, Joan. *What Was the Gold Rush?* New York: Grosset & Dunlap, 2013.

Websites

To learn more about Daily Life in US History, visit **booklinks.abdopublishing.com**. These links are routinely monitored and updated to provide the most current information available.

Visit **www.mycorelibrary.com** for free additional tools for teachers and students.

INDEX

ABOUT THE AUTHOR

Bethany Onsgard works in publishing and spends her days reading, writing, and exploring the outdoors in beautiful Portland, Oregon.